Romana Romanyshyn and Andriy Lesiv

Translated by Vitaly Chernetsky

I See That

At first it was dark, you could not see anything.

We can see thanks to light. Reflecting off objects around us, light gets into our eyes, and our brain transforms it into visual images.

And then light appeared.*

For a few days after birth our picture of the world is fuzzy and turned upside down. Later our brain learns to turn the image it receives right side up.

Eye color depends on the coloring of the eye's iris, and specifically from it containing a pigment called melanin.

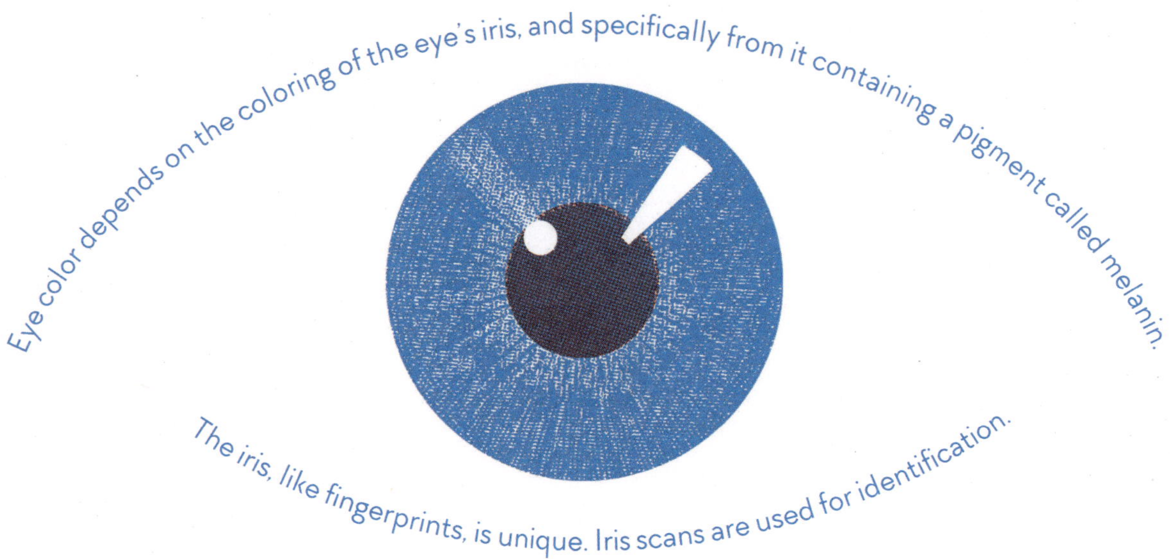

The iris, like fingerprints, is unique. Iris scans are used for identification.

A new day begins.
I open my eyes and see.

So many interesting things in my field of vision.

Approximately 1% of people have the right and the left eye of different colors.
The rarest eye color is green: only about 2% of people on our planet have green eyes.

Sight is the most important sense for humans. About 40% of the cerebral cortex works on processing the information we receive thanks to sight.

E

F P

T O Z

L P E D

P E C F D

E D F C Z P

F E L O P Z D

D E F P O T E C

L E F O D P C T

P E Z O L C F T D

The eye chart tests visual acuity.

The ophthalmologist is a doctor who knows everything about our eyes and vision.

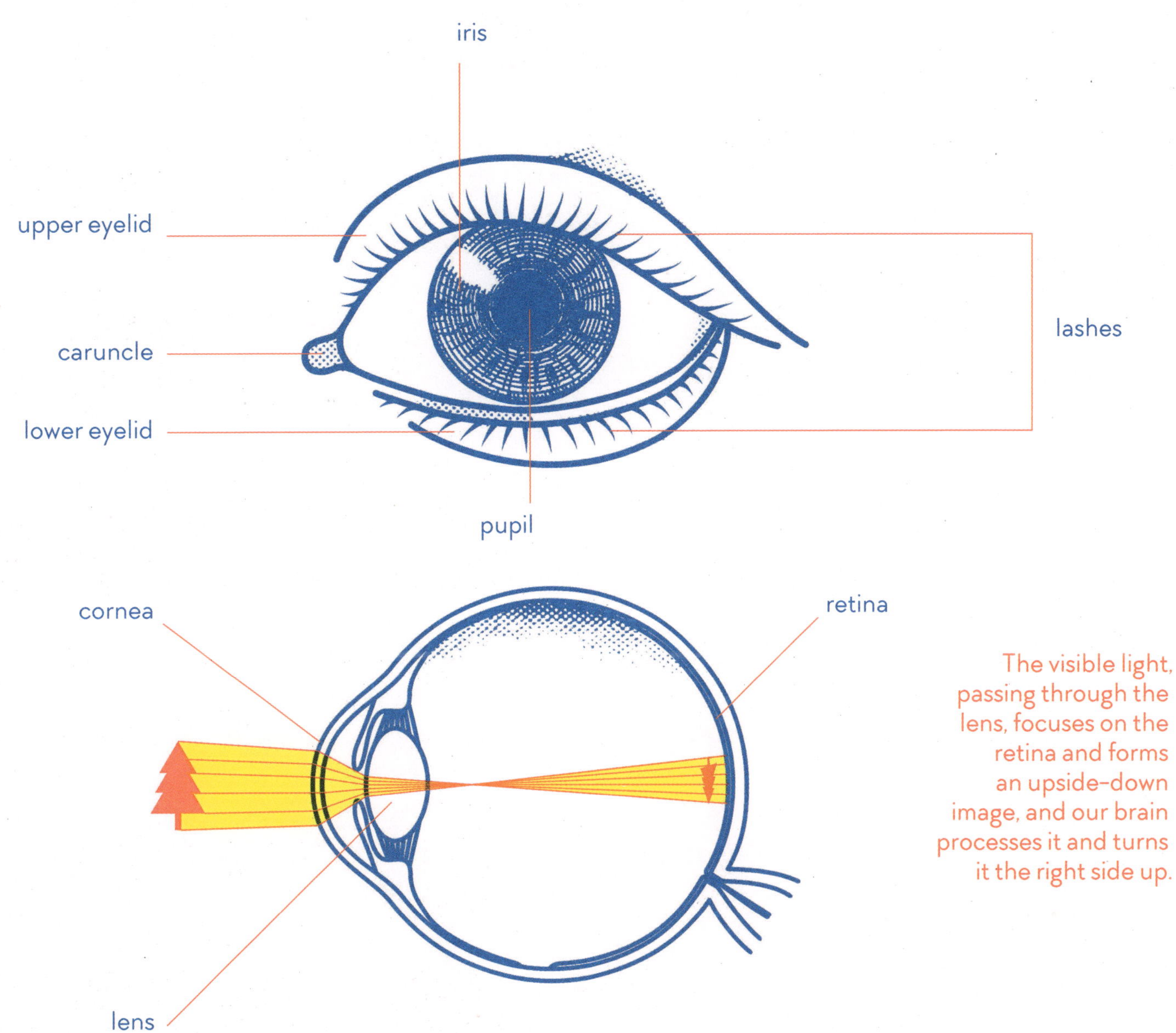

The visible light, passing through the lens, focuses on the retina and forms an upside-down image, and our brain processes it and turns it the right side up.

My eyes are a delicate and complex mechanism.
They notice the tiniest details and show me the big picture of the world.

There are three primary colors: yellow, blue, and red; they cannot be made out of other colors.
Mixing these colors, we get the secondary ones.
snow
coal
cream
seafoam white
lemon
ochre
peach
saffron
cadmium yellow
gold
burnt orange
carrot
sand
powder pink
nude
apricot
salmon
coral
vermilion
carmine
bordeaux
burgundy
aquamarine
mint
cerulean
verdigris
turquoise
teal
ultramarine
cobalt blue
cornflower blue
azure
cherry blossom pink
rose
strawberry
pink flamingo
raspberry
titian
fuchsia
cardinal
magenta
umber
ivory
champagne
cappuccino
taupe
chamois
terracotta
cocoa
chocolate
sepia
bistre
lime
sage
chartreuse
pistachio
olive
emerald
jade
forest
khaki
hunter
periwinkle
lavender
lilac
orchid
violet
amethyst
plum
eggplant
iris
indigo

These seven colors are the colors of the spectrum; we also see them in the rainbow.

Besides spectral colors, there exist countless other hues, and many of them have official names.

The human eye is capable of distinguishing about 7 million variations of color. On average a person can see several hundred thousand hues. The largest number—several million hues—can be seen by visual artists.

Colors can strongly influence our emotions. They can make us happy or sad, calm us, or even make us hungry. Yellow and orange increase one's appetite. Red attracts our attention and warns about danger. Blue provides a feeling of harmony and safety, and green is associated with nature and health.

The condition when a person cannot perceive or distinguish one or more colors is called color blindness or Daltonism.

It is impossible to count all the colors, hues, and tints my eyes can see!

The first mirrors were made of silver, copper, or bronze as far back as the 3rd to 1st millennium B.C. The surface of such mirrors was produced by polishing for a long time, but it gradually darkened and lost the capacity to reflect.

I see myself in the mirror,
I study my face carefully and know its tiniest details.

Later people learned to make mirrors out of glass, adding to its surface a thin layer of metal—silver, gold, or tin.

Today mirrors are manufactures using similar principles.

Funhouse mirrors, convex and concave, create funny distorted images.

To read this, use a mirror.

However, the reflection does not always show who I really am.

I see you and recognize your face among millions of others.

Facial expressions
movements of facial muscles that express a person's feelings and emotions. Facial expressions are extremely important in human communication. When we smile, we show friendliness, and when we frown, we show disagreement or sadness.

Although faces can sometimes seem similar, each of them is unique. But besides us, faces can also be distinguished by technological devices, such as security cameras or modern smartphones which use facial scans to recognize their owners.

Underneath the skin of each person's face there are 43 muscles that express the entire range of our emotions.

From the very first sight I understand whether you are happy or sad.

Good eyesight and attention give us the possibility to see the difference between objects that are identical in shape.

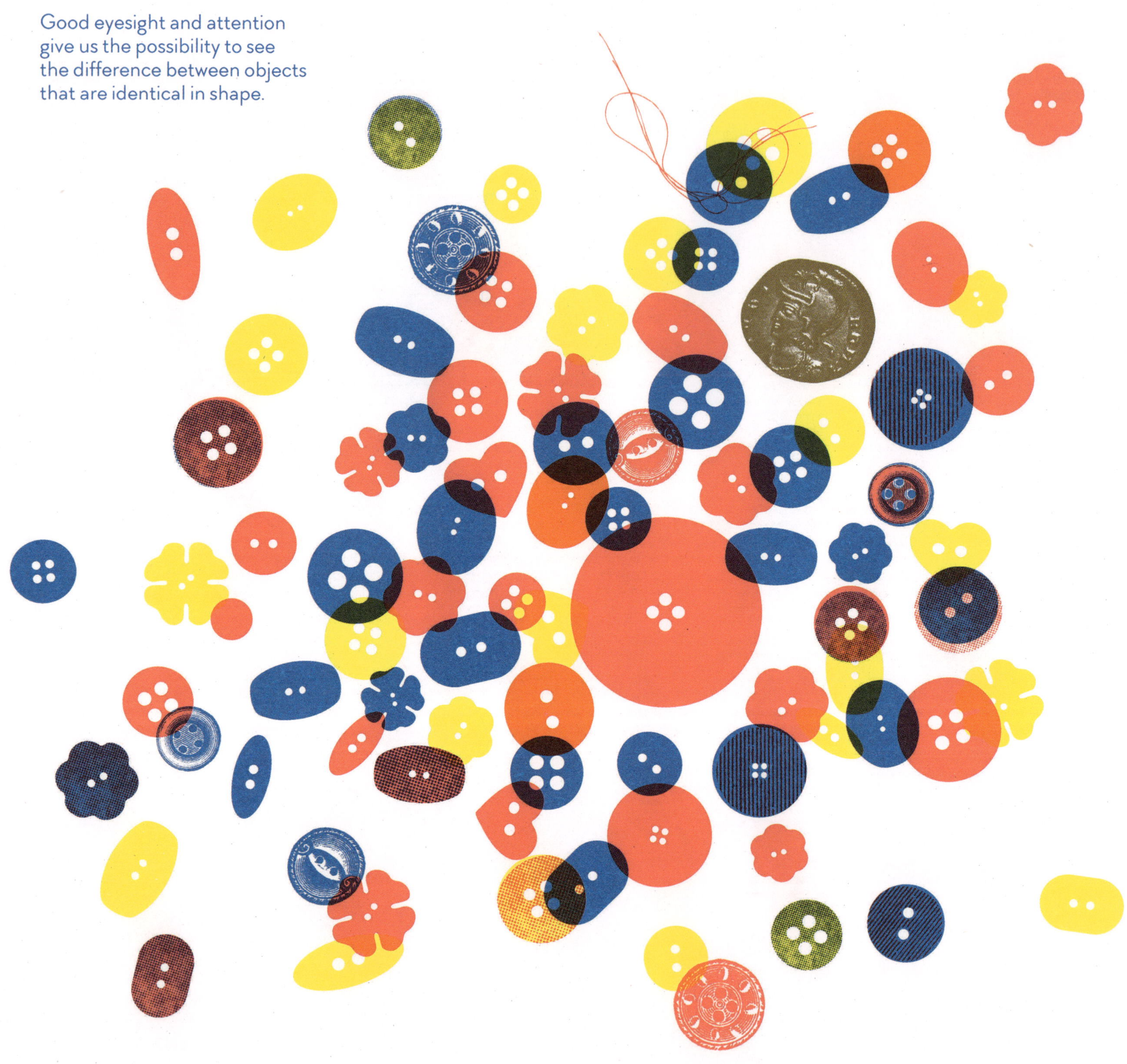

Eyes help me find true treasures

and save me from danger.

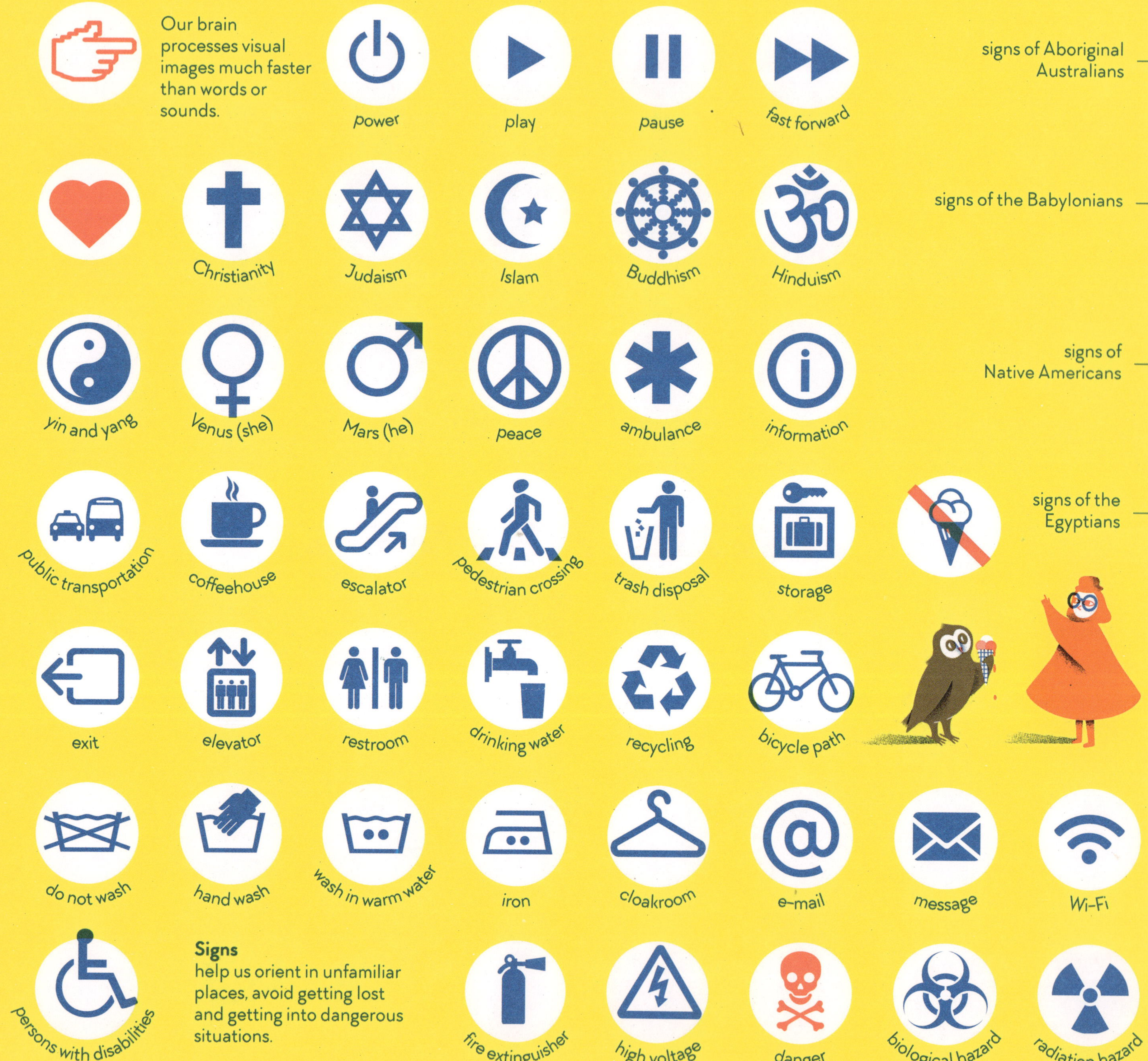

I see signs and symbols that speak to me without words.

boomerang
star
rainbow
mountains
four persons at a table
rain
path
journey

fire
walk
heart
bird
grain
look
hand
ears

happy
sad
hunt
friendship
spring
summer
man
woman

city
light
bread
tears
plow
sugarcane
plants
falcon

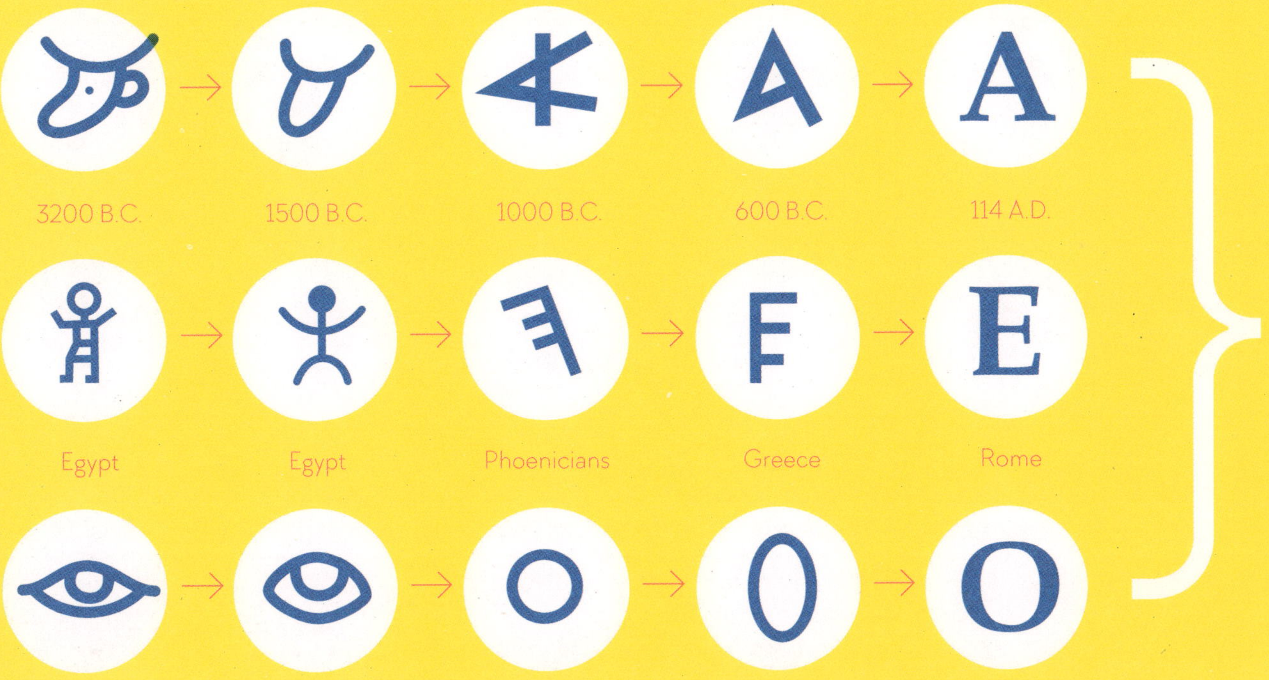

3200 B.C. → 1500 B.C. → 1000 B.C. → 600 B.C. → 114 A.D.

Egypt → Egypt → Phoenicians → Greece → Rome

Pictograms
signs that denote a certain image or notion are the oldest form of communication.

The letters of modern alphabets also developed from ancient pictographic signs.

Pictographic writing
the ancient form of writing used by the civilizations of Mesopotamia, Egypt, China, and others.

I read and decipher them.

Sometimes eyes need help.**

I put on eyeglasses. I look really good in them.

The optical power of lenses is measured in **diopters**.

Virtual reality glasses augment visible reality with holographic images, are controlled by the movement of the eyes, and also by hand gestures and voice commands.

Anaglyph glasses with lenses of two different colors. They are used for looking at stereoscopic images.

Snow goggles the glasses used by the Inuit to protect the eyes from snow blindness. They are made out of wood, walrus tusks, or caribou antlers.

Pince-nez Eyeglasses without earpieces, held on the nose with the help of a spring mechanism.

Monocle is one round lens in a frame, held in the eye socket between the cheek and the eyebrow.

Lorgnette is a pair of grasses in a frame with a special handle. The lorgnette is held by the hand in front of the eyes.

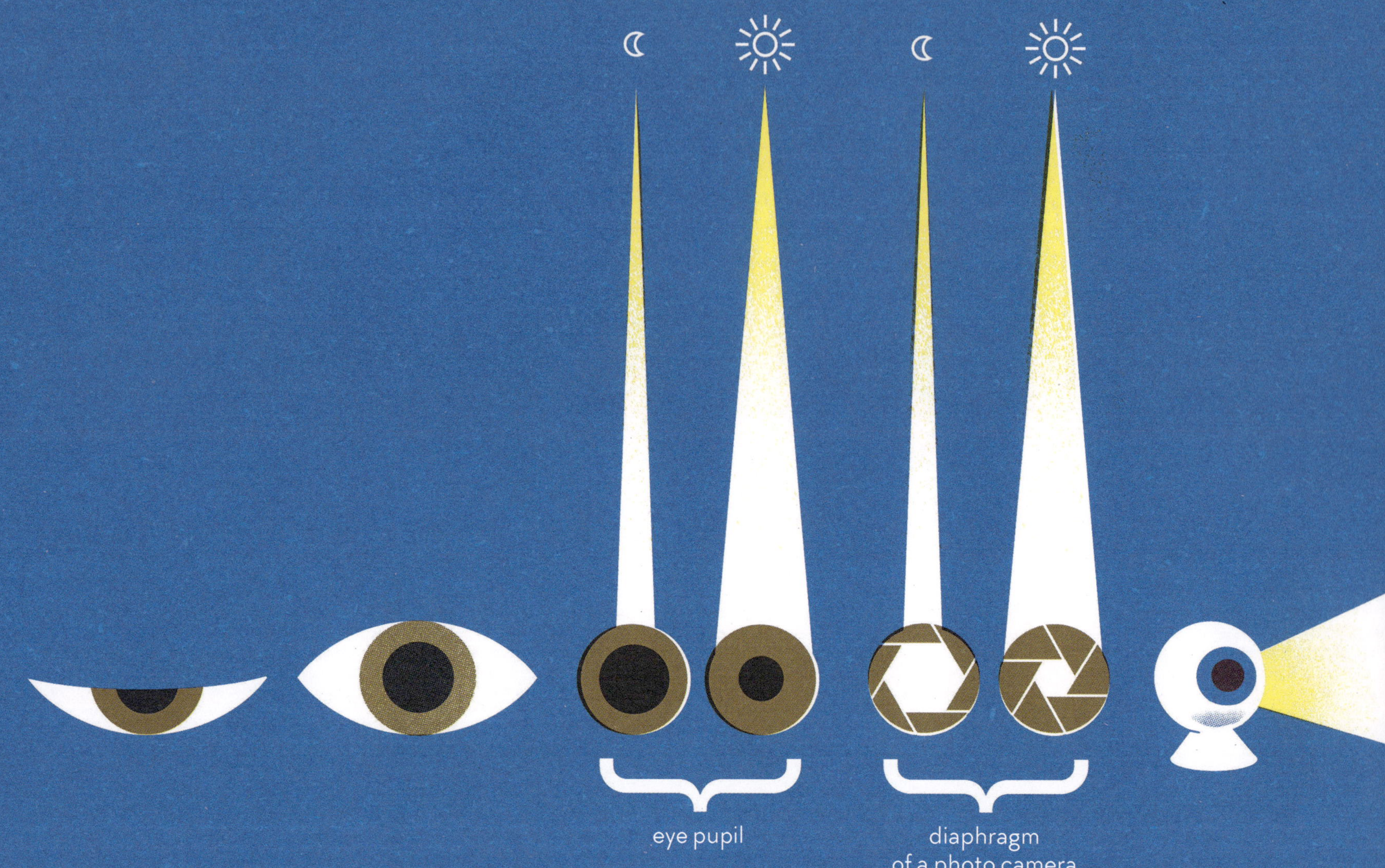

The pupil of the eye works like the diaphragm of a photo camera: in a weekly lit environment the pupil opens to let in more light, and when the lighting is bright, the pupil narrows.

The pupils also open when we see the person we love.

I look at the world with wide open eyes. I yearn to discover the unknown, to see beyond the horizon, to understand things that are not self-evident.

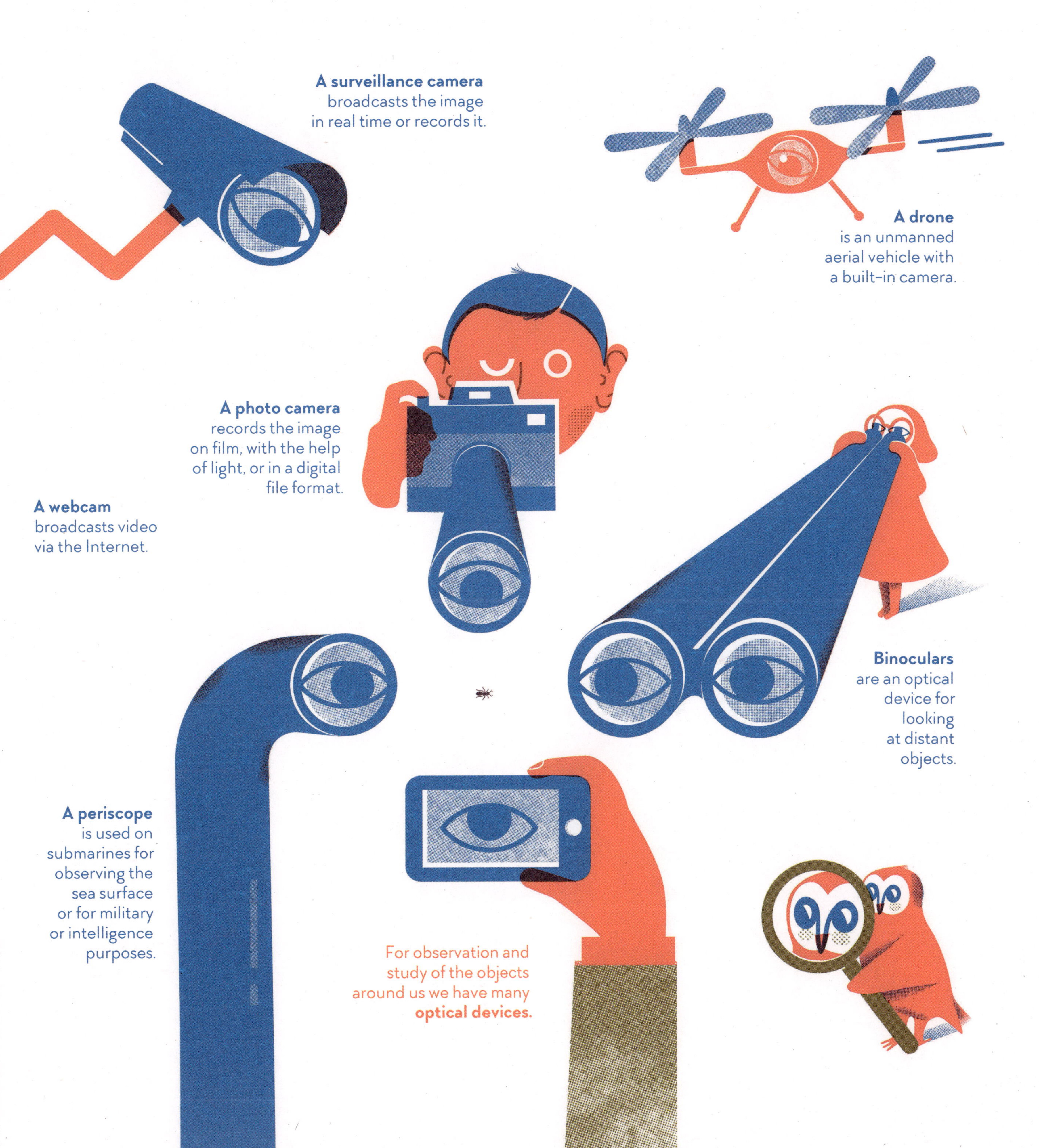

A surveillance camera
broadcasts the image
in real time or records it.
A drone
is an unmanned
aerial vehicle with
a built-in camera.
A photo camera
records the image
on film, with the help
of light, or in a digital
file format.
A webcam
broadcasts video
via the Internet.
Binoculars
are an optical
device for
looking
at distant
objects.
A periscope
is used on
submarines for
observing the
sea surface
or for military
or intelligence
purposes.
For observation and
study of the objects
around us we have many
optical devices.

A microscope is an optical device that makes it possible to see very small objects and details, invisible to the naked eye. It was invented in the late 16th century. Different kinds of microscopes give us the possibility to see the impressive microscopic world of the smallest organisms, bacteria and viruses.

An optical microscope works on the basis of the principle of light refraction by a system of lenses and can magnify an image up to 3 thousand times.

An electron microscope invented in the 1930s, produces an enlarged image with the help of beams of electrons, and can magnify an image tens and hundreds of thousands of times.

Incredibly small objects seem surprisingly large.

And things that are extremely far away seem exceptionally close.

Atoms
everything that is around us, including ourselves, is built out of atoms, but they are so tiny that they cannot be seen even with the most powerful microscope.

Air
we live thanks to air, we breathe oxygen that is contained in it, but we cannot see it.

Gravitation
if there were no gravitation, we would freely bounce around the Universe. We can measure it, but we cannot see it.

Dark matter
80% of the Universe is dark matter. It cannot be seen, but we know that it exists. All the planets, stars, galaxies—everything that we can see—makes up only one fifth of the Universe; the rest is invisible.

A black hole
the gravitation of a black hole is so powerful that even light cannot escape it, therefore it cannot be seen.

However, there are still so many mysteries for my eyes.

Thoughts
we can observe the brain
and chemical reactions within it,
but thoughts remain invisible.

Soul
it is impossible to see a soul,
but one can believe in its existence.

Some things remain invisible.

Optical illusions
are errors of our visual perception. In contemporary art there is a separate movement based on optical illusions: op art.***

An illusionist
is an artist who demonstrates tricks, creates illusions, manipulating the viewers' attention.

One of the most famous illusion drawings, **"Duck or Rabbit,"** was created in 1892.

The Japanese psychologist Akiyoshi Kitaoka creates and studies optical illusions that seem to move and look similar to this one.

Sometimes sight deceives me.
Stay focused, pay attention to details—then everything will become clear.

Camouflage
use of color to hide or disguise

Mimicry
chameleons, octopuses, and cuttlefish change their color depending on their surroundings and this way become hard to notice.

Flounder and halibut are fish that imitate the color of the sea floor.

Spots, dots, and stripes on animal fur help animals be less noticeable.

The mountain hare changes its fur color to white in winter, and then back to dark in springtime.

It is very hard to see someone who hides well.

Actually, everyone wants to hide sometimes.

There are eyes that see better than mine.

Flies and some other insects have special complex eyes that are called multifaceted or compound eyes. They are built out of multiple separate individual lenses.

The eye of an **eagle** is about the same size as a human eye but sees approximately eight times sharper and better.

Goats, sheep, and **mongoose** have rectangular horizontal pupils, thanks to which their field of vision reaches 340 degrees.

The eyes of a **rat**, like those of a chameleon, move independently from one another in different directions.

Tarsiers have the largest eyes compared to the size of their bodies out of all the mammals. Thanks to this they see very well in daylight and at night, and also in ultraviolet light.

The eyes of a **chameleon** move independently from one another in different directions. Thanks to that chameleons have a full 360-degree field of vision.

Owls have sharp eyesight, and see well at great distances both in daylight and at night.

The eyes of a **shark** are very sensitive to light; sharks see well even in dark and cloudy water.

The eye of a **butterfly** has 15 photoreceptors. By comparison, the human eye has only three.

Even in the dark.

A **fly**
sees the image as if put together from many little pieces, like a puzzle, and its field of vision is almost 360 degrees.

An **owl**
sees very well in the dark and has very sharp eyesight but distinguishes fewer colors than humans.

A **horse** and a **zebra**
have very wide peripheral vision, but horses have a blind spot in front of their noses because their eyes are placed on the sides of their heads. They can distinguish blue and green hues but mostly see shades of grey.

A **cat**,
just like a dog, sees fewer colors—mostly browns, yellows, and blues. Cats have a wider field of vision than humans—approximately 200 degrees.

A **dog**
has much wider peripheral vision than a human but sees fewer colors. A dog's eye distinguishes mostly shades of brown, blue, and yellow.

So interesting to see the world through your eyes.

But seeing is not only the sense of sight.

Hearing
sounds help us orient in space. People who are visually impaired rely on their hearing, on the auditory environment, and echolocation.

Smell
we sense lots of different smells. And it is smell that is a strong trigger of memories.

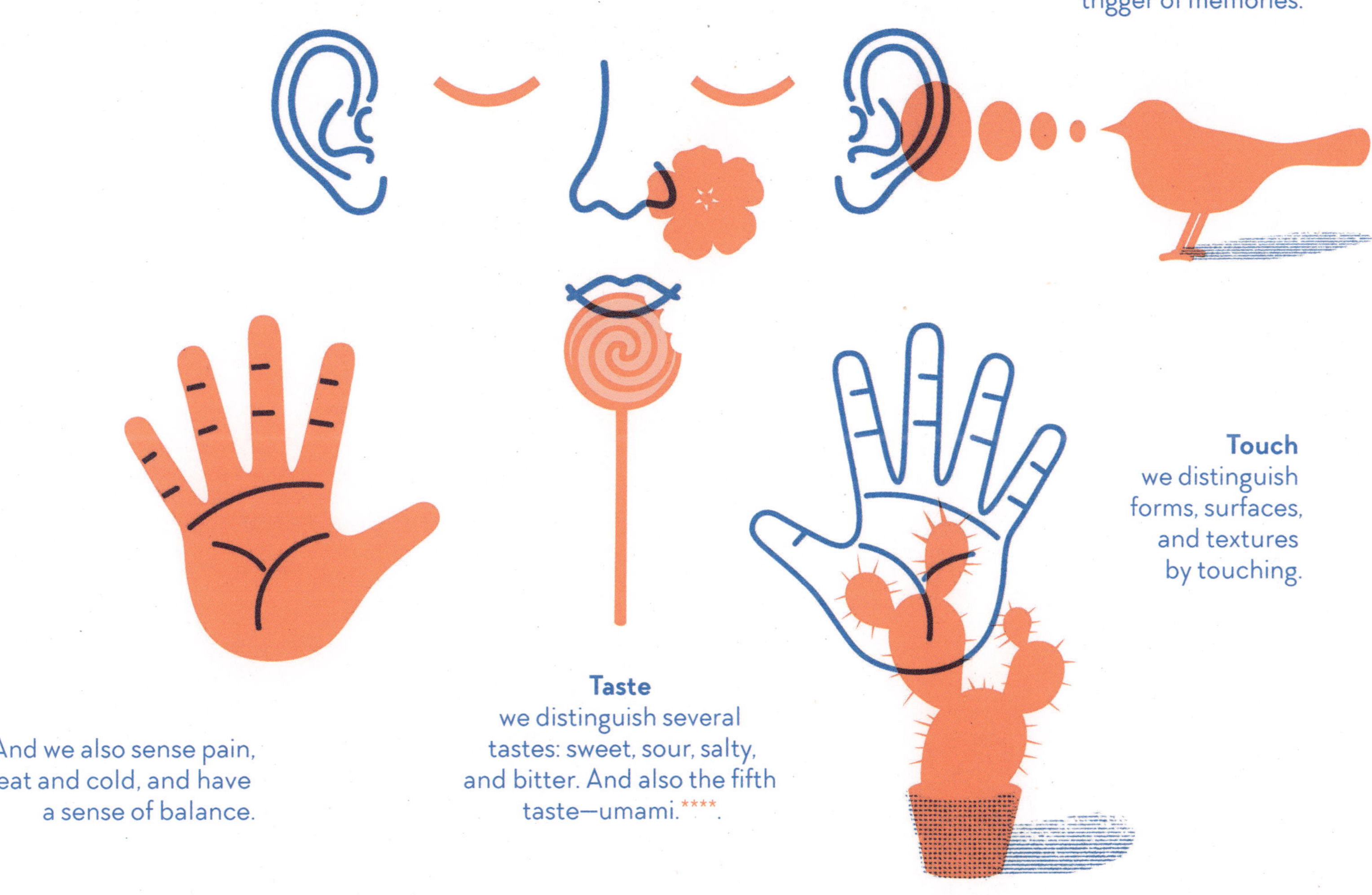

Touch
we distinguish forms, surfaces, and textures by touching.

Taste
we distinguish several tastes: sweet, sour, salty, and bitter. And also the fifth taste—umami.****.

And we also sense pain, heat and cold, and have a sense of balance.

**I see more than what my eyes can see.
And senses help me explore the world around me.**

A white cane with a red tip
it is hard to orient in space without seeing. This is why people who are visually impaired use a cane to identify obstacles when walking. The white cane was introduced in France by Guilly d'Herbemont in 1931.

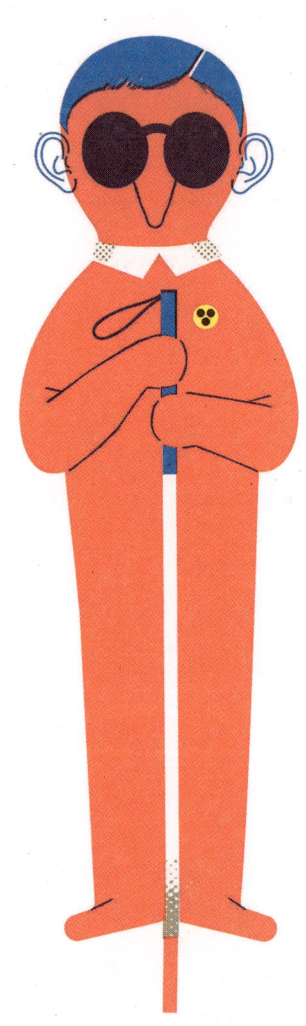

Some live without seeing but sense all the colors of the world.

For safe movement blind persons use GPS systems that mark precise location with sound signals.

Blind people are also aided by guide dogs. These dogs are specially selected and trained to help people. The breeds that are recognized as most suited for this work are Golden Retrievers and Labradors.

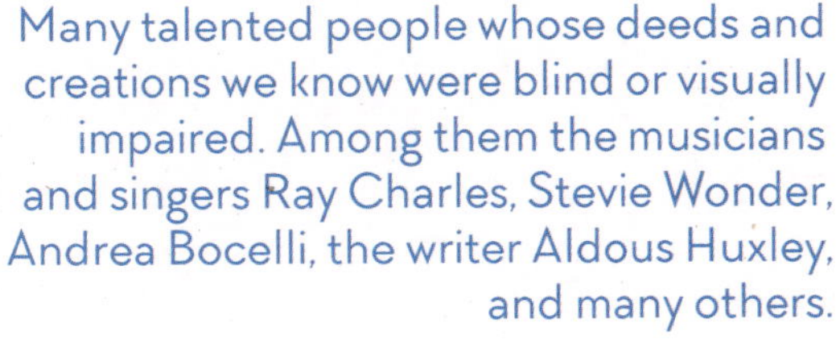

Many talented people whose deeds and creations we know were blind or visually impaired. Among them the musicians and singers Ray Charles, Stevie Wonder, Andrea Bocelli, the writer Aldous Huxley, and many others.

Bumps in the form of long stripes and round dots on sidewalks help visually impaired people avoid obstacles and dangers in their path. They are often marked with contrasting colors.

This system was developed in Japan in the 1960s.

The raised long stripes mark the direction of movement, and the dots inform about a change: a turn, a staircase, an obstacle ahead, etc.

Sounds, smells, and textures help travel,

not get lost, and always find the way home.

Braille
is a script for reading and writing developed for the visually impaired by the Frenchman Louis Braille in 1829; he was only 15 years old then.

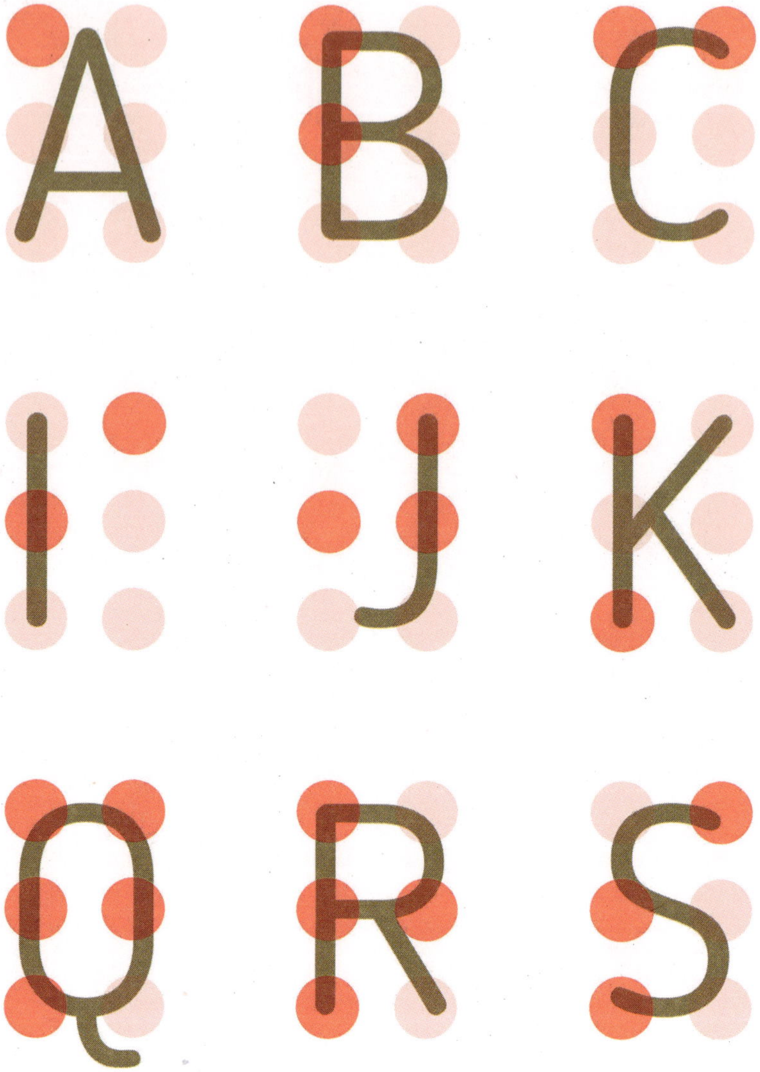

A B C

I J K

Q R S

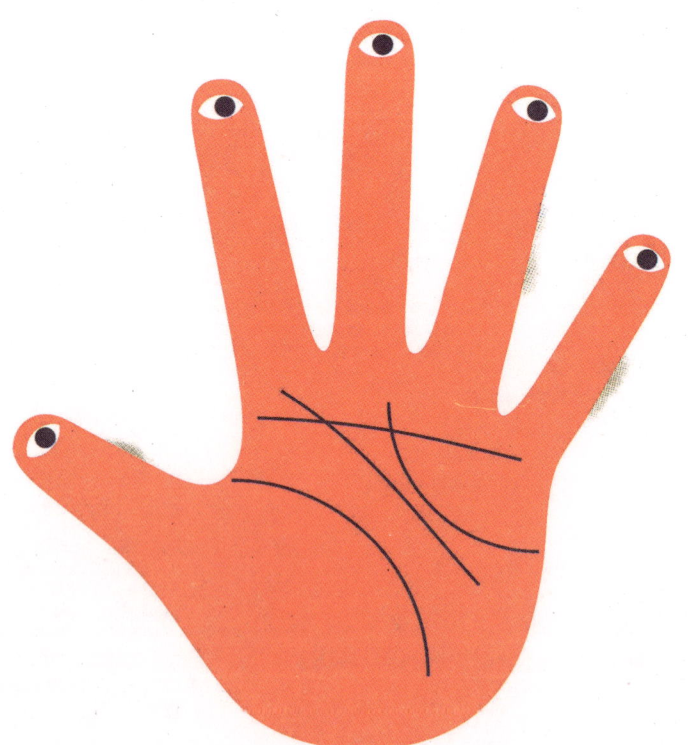

The 6 dots of Braille create 64 possible combinations for marking different letters, numbers, and symbols.

The basis for the writing system is a matrix of six dots. Depending on the letter, the necessary dots in the matrix are raised so that they could be sensed by touch.

Only six dots suffice to say so much.

Posing for a photographer was once considered a special occasion that demanded thorough preparation and time. This is why on old photos everyone looks serious and imposing. Today for us photos are mostly a mundane thing; we take dozens of photos every day.

I again look through old memories. And create new ones.

A shot from the film Earth (1930) by the Ukrainian director Alexander Dovzhenko, a famous masterpiece of world cinema.

Cinema
is the sequence of individual photographic shots that replace one another at the speed of 24 frames per second. It is precisely at this speed that our eye stops noticing the replacement of static shots and sees a smooth moving cinematic picture.

Typhlocomments
a voice in the earphone comments for the visually impaired person what is happening on the screen.

With each new shot on the screen I learn a new story.

Contemplation of beauty makes a strong impact on us. Beautiful things attract our gaze; we hold our breath, are lost for words, we can even get teary-eyed because of beauty.

Aesthetics
is a branch of scholarship that explores what is beautiful, the sensory exploration of the world, and the nature of beauty.

"What do you see?"

"On the painting there are four figures in multicolored clothes and shoes. They stand up straight against the background of an endless field behind which there is a narrow strip of water. To me it looks like the sea."

In Japanese culture it is believed that contemplating nature brings a person closer to grasping the principles of life. Nature does not have things that are not beautiful. This is why in Japanese buildings a window that has a nice view is often framed as a picture, and the landscape is perceived as an exquisite work of art in and of itself.

and find it even in simple things around me.

I have lots of ideas.
In my imagination I picture
what I have not seen yet.

I change the point of view
in order to see more.

Look at this image from far away *****

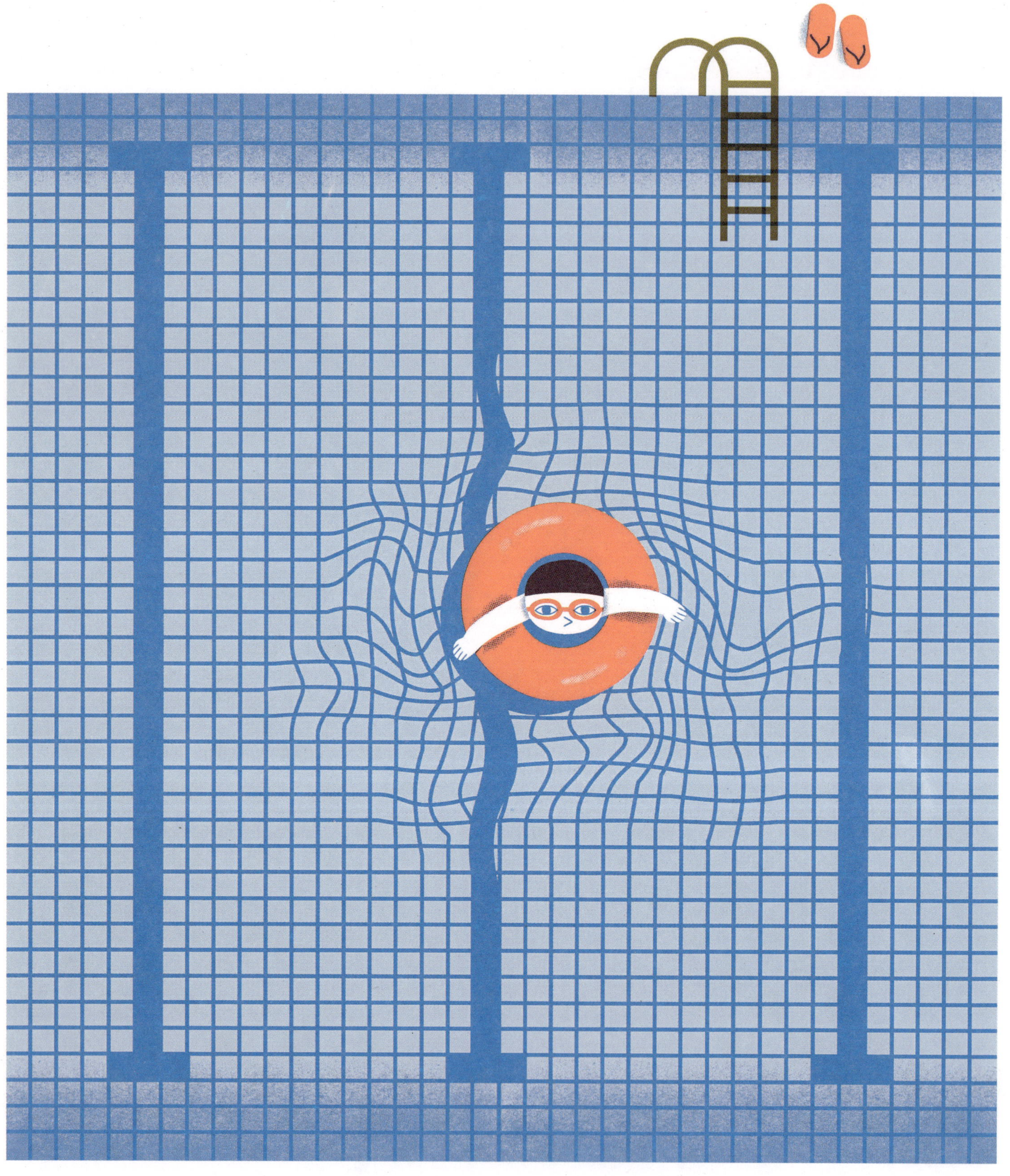

Every day I learn something new and look at the world as if for the first time.

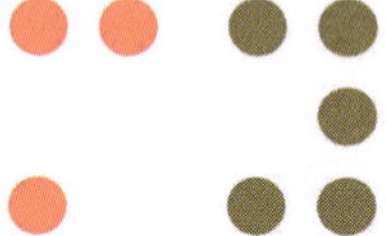

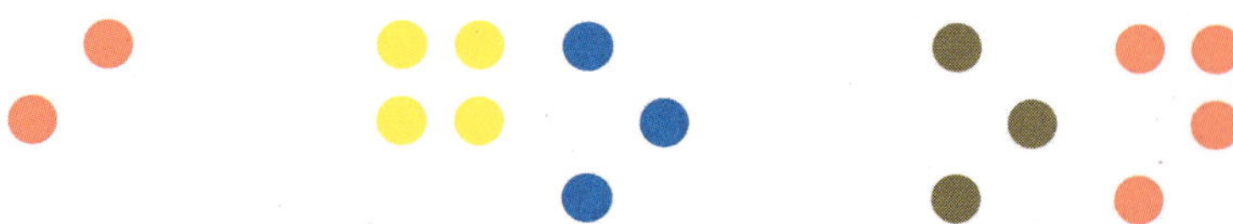

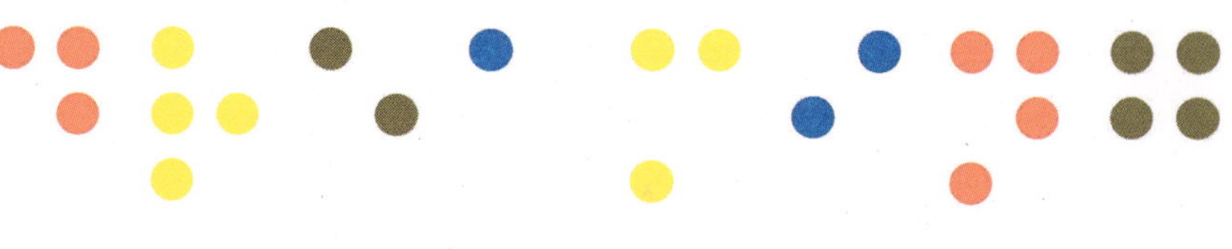

Ursa Major

Orion

Cassiopeia

Leo

Andromeda

And see dreams.

For sale in Indian Subcontinent only

Wonder House Books is an imprint of
Prakash Books India Pvt. Ltd.
Canada | India

Originally published in 2017 under the title "я так бачу"
by Vydavnytstvo Staroho Leva (The Old Lion Publishing House), Lviv, Ukraine.